HOW DID THAT GET TO MY HOUSE?

HOW DID THAT GET TO MY HOUSE?
WATER

BY NANCY R. MASTERS

COMMUNITY • CONNECTIONS

?

Published in the United States of America by Cherry Lake Publishing
Ann Arbor, Michigan
www.cherrylakepublishing.com

Content Adviser: Colin Brooks, Research Scientist, Michigan Tech Research Institute,
Houghton, Michigan
Reading Adviser: Cecilia Minden-Cupp, PhD, Literacy Consultant

Photo Credits: Cover and pages 1, 5, and 7, ©Paul Brennan, used under license from
Shutterstock, Inc.; pages 9 and 11, ©mmm, used under license from Shutterstock, Inc.;
page 13, ©iStock.com/lambelin; page 15, ©iStock.com/AWSeebaran; page 17,
©Lucian Coman, used under license from Shutterstock, Inc.; page 19, ©iStock.com/DenGuy;
page 21, ©Jirkaejc/Dreamstime.com

LIBRARY OF CONGRESS CATALOGING-IN-PUBLICATION DATA
Masters, Nancy Robinson.
  How did that get to my house? Water / by Nancy Robinson Masters.
      p. cm.—(Community connections)
  Includes index.
  ISBN-13: 978-1-60279-475-7
  ISBN-10: 1-60279-475-8
  1. Water-supply—Juvenile literature. 2. Water—Juvenile literature.
  3. Drinking water—Juvenile literature I. Title. II. Title: Water. III. Series.
  TD348.M38 2010
  628.1—dc22   2008052350

Cherry Lake Publishing would like to acknowledge the
work of The Partnership for 21st Century Skills. Please
visit www.21stcenturyskills.org for more information.

Printed in the United States of America, Corporate Graphics.
March 2010
CLSP06

WATER

CONTENTS

4 **What Is Water?**

10 **Capturing and Storing Water**

16 **Cleaning and Moving Water**

22 Glossary

23 Find Out More

24 Index

24 About the Author

WHAT IS WATER?

Splash! There is water in your bathtub. Swish! There is water in your sink. Gulp! There is water in your cup.

Water is one of Earth's most important **natural resources**. All living things need water. Turning on the **faucet** in your house lets water run indoors.

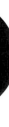

Clean water moves through pipes. It goes to each faucet in your house.

Have you ever wondered where the water in the faucet comes from? It begins with Earth's water cycle. This water cycle includes **evaporation** and **precipitation**. Evaporation happens when the sun's heat changes water into **vapor**. Also, trees drink up rainwater. Trees let vapor into the air through their leaves.

Leaves on trees and other plants let water vapor into the air.

The water vapor rises. Precipitation happens when the air cannot hold any more water vapor. The vapor forms drops as it cools. The drops fall back to Earth as rain, snow, sleet, or hail.

Rainstorms are part of the water cycle.

Look around your house. Find all of the things that use water. How many things did you find? Were most of them in the same room?

CAPTURING AND STORING WATER

Lakes and ponds collect the drops of water. Lakes and ponds are a natural resource. People also build **reservoirs**. Reservoirs capture and store water. They are easier to control than natural lakes. This is because people can control the flow of a reservoir's water.

Dams are built to hold back water and store it in reservoirs.

Some water soaks into the ground. This water is held underground between layers of rock called **aquifers**. An aquifer can hold and store millions of gallons of water. Aquifers have been holding and storing water for millions of years. Some people build wells to get water from aquifers.

This old well uses a bucket on a chain to get water.

Not all water is stored in lakes or reservoirs. People in cities and towns build **water towers**. These big tanks store an extra supply of water.

Water towers come in all shapes and sizes. They are easy to see because they are tall. The reason they are tall is so the water will easily flow down when needed.

14

Pumps are used to fill water towers.

Water towers can hold as much water as 50 swimming pools. How much water do you think your bathtub can hold? Can you think of a way to find out?

CLEANING AND MOVING WATER

People in some parts of the world must travel very far to find water. They carry the water back to their homes in pots or buckets. This water may be unclean. It might contain dirt and germs that cause sickness.

Some people live where there are no pipes to bring water to homes. Why do you think they are careful not to waste water?

In other countries, **water treatment plants** clean water. They remove trash and dirt and kill germs.

Pumps move clean water into storage tanks. Large pipes carry this water to smaller pipes. These underground pipes spread out like a spider web. They carry water to each house.

Water treatment plants use huge pumps to move water.

POTABLE WATER

Pipes in your house are called plumbing. Plumbing carries clean water in and used water out.

People can't live without water. Water tanks and pipes make it easy for some people to get clean water. Maybe someday people everywhere will have pipes bringing clean water to their homes.

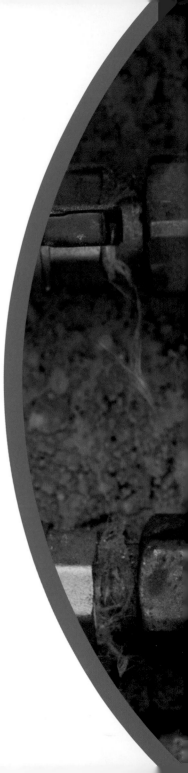

People in most towns must pay for the water they use. Water meters measure how much water is used in a house.

Ask an adult to show you the water meter at your house. The meter keeps track of how much water you use. Talk about ways you can save water.

GLOSSARY

aquifers (AH-kwih-furz) layers of rock that capture and hold water underground

evaporation (ih-vap-uh-RAY-shuhn) the process of a liquid changing into a vapor or gas

faucet (FAW-sit) a handle attached to a valve that controls the flow of water

natural resources (NACH-urh-uhl REE-sor-sez) things in nature that humans can use

precipitation (pri-sip-i-TAY-shuhn) water from the sky in the form of rain, snow, sleet, or hail

reservoirs (REZ-uh-vwarz) places built to store water

vapor (VAY-pur) tiny drops of water, that hang in the air

water towers (WAW-tur TOU-urz) tall tanks used to store water

water treatment plants (WAW-tur TREET-muhnt PLANTS) places where water is cleaned

FIND OUT MORE

BOOKS

Bailey, Jacqui, and Matthew Lilly. *A Drop in the Ocean: The Story of Water*. Minneapolis: Picture Window Books, 2004.

Green, Jen. *How the Water Cycle Works*. New York: PowerKids Press, 2008.

WEB SITES

The Story of Drinking Water

www.bgmukids.com/story_of_water/html/story.htm
Facts and games about drinking water and water treatment plants

Water Towers

www.watertowers.com
All about water towers, with facts and photos of famous water towers in the world

INDEX

aquifers, 12

cities, 14

dirt, 16, 18

evaporation, 6

faucets, 4, 6

germs, 16, 18

hail, 8

lakes, 10

natural resources, 4, 10

pipes, 18, 20
plumbing, 20
ponds, 10

precipitation, 6, 8
pumps, 18

rain, 6, 8
reservoirs, 10

sickness, 16
sleet, 8
snow, 8

towns, 14
trees, 6

vapor, 6, 8

water cycle, 6
water meters, 21
water tanks, 18, 20
water towers, 14, 15
water treatment plants, 18

ABOUT THE AUTHOR

Nancy Robinson Masters once lived in a house that did not have running water. She is glad that she now lives in a house that does. Drinking water helps her read and write books.